Lives of the Artists

LIVES
OF THE
ARTISTS

M. B. Goffstein

Farrar · Straus · Giroux

New York

To my parents,
Esther and Albert Goffstein

Contents

REMBRANDT

VAN RIJN

1606–1669

Rembrandt van Rijn / *The Artist in His Studio* / circa 1628

Oil on panel / 10 × 12½ inches (25.4 × 31.8 cm)

Museum of Fine Arts, Boston

Zoe Oliver Sherman Collection

Artists,

whether great or small,

give away their beauty,

and crave the work

of other minds

to feed their hungry eyes.

The greatest artist

of them all

was Rembrandt.

He had the largest appetite

for works of every kind.

One small tin pot

told him,

"You are not alone.

I am humble, too."

Twenty marble heads

of Roman emperors said,

"Once we were great

like you."

"You can be like us,"

said the paintings.

Two exclaimed:

"Raphael will never die

as long as we survive!"

"We seem to be miracles,

yet we led simple lives,"

said the seashells.

And the ancient weapons

and wind instruments

sighed,

"All land and sea creatures

lead simple lives

of great mystery."

One large mirror

silently agreed,

in Rembrandt's home

in Amsterdam.

Every outside

has an inside,

and every inside

has an outside.

Just one stroke

of Rembrandt's

chalk,

needle, brush, or pen

could tell both tales.

They tell them

to this day.

Rembrandt van Rijn / *Woman Teaching a Child to Stand* / circa 1637

Red chalk / 3⅟₁₆ × 2¹⁵⁄₁₆ inches (7.8 × 7.5 cm)

The British Museum, London

FRANCESCO

GUARDI

1712 — 1793

Francesco Guardi / *Architectural Fantasy* / circa 1780

Oil on canvas / 12⅜ × 10⅝ inches (31.4 × 27 cm)

The Metropolitan Museum of Art, New York

Bequest of Emma A. Sheafer, 1974 / The Lesley and Emma Sheafer Collection

Guardi,

we don't know

too much about you.

Your sister wed

Tiepolo.

Your father,

your two brothers,

and your sons

were painters, too.

In your own time

Canaletto

was acknowledged master

of the Venetian view.

Canaletto

stood on the Rialto,

looking at the houses

through a camera obscura.

He drew them in perspective

with a compass

and a ruler.

His highways of green water

and their reflective twin,

the skies,

were brushed dramatically.

That was not true of you,

Guardi.

Rows of buildings

on the lagoon

seemed to dance

before your eyes,

and their balcony railings

looked like the notes

to tunes

that flew away

from music paper.

Venice was made

on mushy land.

Laws changed,

and people died.

Guardi,

you must have dreamed

about the sky,

where order reigned.

Every little faraway cloud

you painted

has stronger architecture

than any home

on the canal.

Francesco Guardi / *The Ponte dei Sospiri* / date unknown

Pen and brown ink / 7 × 3¾ inches (17.8 × 9.4 cm)

Galleria Uffizi, Florence

VINCENT

VAN GOGH

1853–1890

Vincent van Gogh / *Self-portrait with Gray Felt Hat* / 1887

Oil on cardboard / 7½ × 5½ inches (19 × 14 cm)

Rijksmuseum Vincent van Gogh, Amsterdam

Respect the speckled things

in nature:

the freckled arm

beneath the surgeon's

short-sleeved gown,

the eggs of birds,

their fuzzy young,

and the Dutch painter

Vincent van Gogh,

red, rough, gruff,

yet very tender.

The green caterpillar

he returned to a tree

did not hurt him either,

nor the starving dog

he fed.

But he was hurt

by people.

And like the combination

of oil and turpentine

painters use,

he too

was a dangerous mixture

which might craze or crack.

He tried to stay away

from people,

even from his brother,

Theo.

Lonely, ill, and poor,

he seemed to be

accursed in every way.

But was his misery

like dust,

purposely kicked up

to keep all jealous eyes

from his brushstrokes

of whirling beauty?

He rarely signed his art.

He once said:

"They will recognize my work

later on,

and write about me

when I'm dead and gone."

Harsh, rejoicing lines

of arm or leaf or stem

signify

that they were made

by Vincent's hand.

Vincent van Gogh / *Town Hall of Auvers* / 1890

Black chalk / 9¼ × 12¼ inches (23.5 × 31 cm)

Rijksmuseum Vincent van Gogh, Amsterdam

PIERRE

BONNARD

1867 – 1947

Pierre Bonnard / *Woman and Dog* / 1922

Oil on canvas / 27 × 15½ inches (68.6 × 39.4 cm)

The Phillips Collection, Washington, D.C.

I did not go to Le Cannet

and climb the steps

to "Le Bosquet,"

where Bonnard lived

with his dachshund,

Poucette,

and the lady who liked

to take baths,

but I've been there.

The luncheon table

is always set,

and the clean lady sits still

in her chair,

red hair bent over

the dog's red fur,

above the white cloth

where the wine bottle stands,

and grapes and cheese—

I can see them.

The golden sun and the trees

and vines,

trying hard to get inside,

press themselves flat

at the windows.

Scratch, scratch, scratch,

Bonnard made notes

in pencil, on paper.

Later, alone

in his small gray room,

he painted those things

he saw every day

and loved to remember.

Around and around

went Bonnard's brush,

touching oil paint

to his canvas.

Around and around

went Bonnard's brush,

dipped in one color,

then another and another—

until the scene

seemed to be reflected

in a silver candy wrapper.

This is the way

the tall, thin, shy man

has invited us in.

Though he has gone,

we can stay there.

Pierre Bonnard / *View from the Artist's Window* / circa 1938

Pencil, studio stamp / 7 × 4⅝ inches (17.8 × 11.7 cm)

Collection of Alfred Ayrton, Monte Carlo

LOUISE

NEVELSON

1900—

Louise Nevelson / *Sky Cathedral* / 1958

Wood construction painted black / 135½ × 120¼ × 18 inches (344 × 305.4 × 45.7 cm)

The Museum of Modern Art, New York / Gift of Mr. and Mrs. Ben Mildwoff

Louise Nevelson

took a shipbuilder's name,

and the things she makes

are seaworthy.

The wooden refuse

of New York City's streets,

of the sea,

lumberyard scraps,

and lathe-turned products

are gathered up by her

and taken home

and painted black as tar.

Years or days later,

or right away,

with a practiced hand

and eye,

they're placed

inside black boxes.

The quiet talk

among the black forms

in each black box

is never-ending.

They are radio receivers

of silence.

Louise Nevelson

wears beautiful clothes:

an early American quilt

made into a skirt,

a denim shirt,

and an emperor's robe

for work or sleeping.

Box upon box

she stacks into walls—

not only black,

but white or gold,

or clear or steel!

Why are the black boxes

whispering?

Of what do the white boxes

sing?

And the golden boxes

proclaim what?

Freedom, equality,

wastefulness, beauty.

Something American!

Louise Berliawsky

sailed to America,

and created American art.

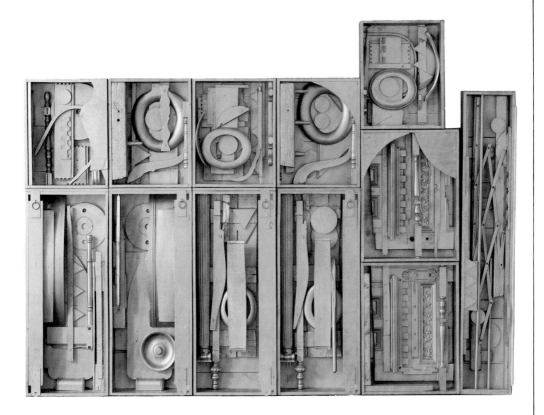

Louise Nevelson / *Royal Tide II* / 1961–1963

Wood construction painted gold / 94½ × 126½ × 8 inches (240 × 321.3 × 20.3 cm)

Whitney Museum of American Art, New York / Gift of the Artist

920
GO

Goffstein, M. B.

Lives of the artists